World Languages

Colors in German

Daniel Nunn

Chicago, Illinois

www.capstonepub.com
Visit our website to find out more information about Heinemann-Raintree books.

To order:
☎ Phone 800-747-4992
💻 Visit www.capstonepub.com to browse our catalog and order online.

Edited by Rebecca Rissman, Dan Nunn, and Sian Smith
Designed by Joanna Hinton-Malivoire
Picture research by Elizabeth Alexander
Production by Alison Parsons
Originated by Capstone Global Library Ltd
Printed and bound in China by South China Printing Company Ltd

16 15 14 13 12
10 9 8 7 6 5 4 3 2 1

Library of Congress Cataloging-in-Publication Data
Nunn, Daniel.
   Colors in German : die farben / Daniel Nunn.
      p. cm.—(World languages - Colors)
   Includes bibliographical references and index.
   ISBN 978-1-4329-6653-9—ISBN 978-1-4329-6660-7 (pbk.) 1. German language—Textbooks for foreign speakers—English—Juvenile literature. 2. Colors—Juvenile literature. I. Title.
   PF3129.E5N86 2013
   438.2′421—dc23   2011046565

Acknowledgments
We would like to thank Shutterstock for permission to reproduce photographs: pp.4 (© Phiseksit), 5 (© Stephen Aaron Rees), 6 (© Tischenko Irina), 7 (© Tony Magdaraog), 8 (© szefei), 9 (© Picsfive), 10 (© Eric Isselée), 11 (© Yasonya), 12 (© Nadezhda Bolotina), 13 (© Maryna Gviazdovska), 14 (© Erik Lam), 15 (© Eric Isselée), 16 (© Ruth Black), 17 (© blueskies9), 18 (© Alexander Dashewsky), 19 (© Michele Perbellini), 20 (© Eric Isselée), 21 (© Roman Rvachov).

Cover photographs reproduced with permission of Shutterstock: dog (© Erik Lam), strawberry (© Stephen Aaron Rees), fish (© Tischenko Irina). Back cover photograph of a banana reproduced with permission of Shutterstock (© Picsfive).

We would like to thank Regina Irwin and Robert Irwin for their invaluable assistance in the preparation of this book.

Every effort has been made to contact copyright holders of material reproduced in this book. Any omissions will be rectified in subsequent printings if notice is given to the publisher.

Contents

Rot

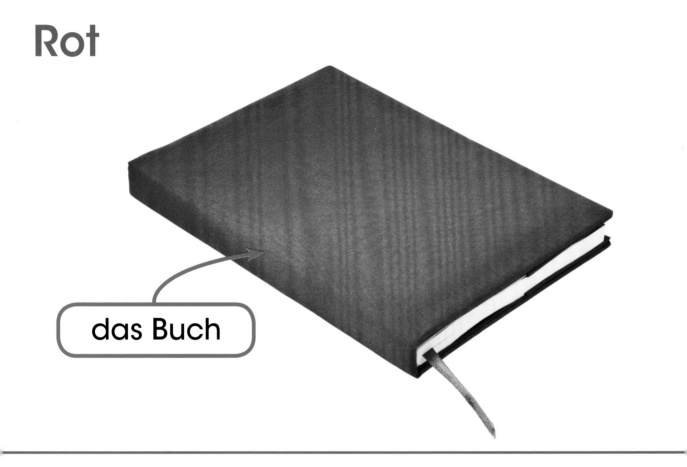

das Buch

Das Buch ist rot.

die Erdbeere

Die Erdbeere ist rot.

Orange

der Fisch

Der Fisch ist orange.

die Karotte

Die Karotte ist orange.

Gelb

die Blume

Die Blume ist gelb.

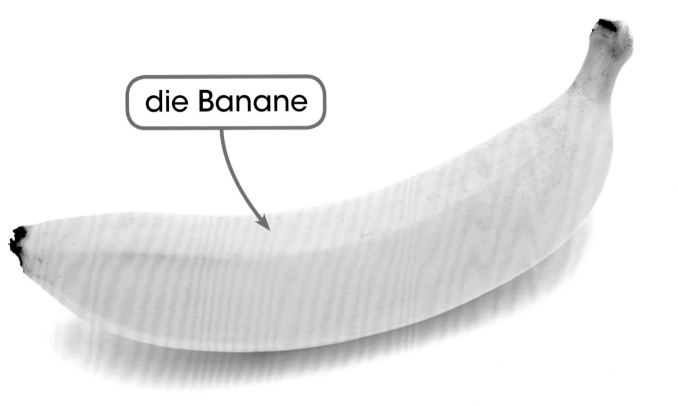

die Banane

Die Banane ist gelb.

Grün

der Vogel

Der Vogel ist grün.

der Apfel

Der Apfel ist grün.

Blau

das T-shirt

Das T-shirt ist blau.

die Tasse

Die Tasse ist blau.

Braun

der Hund

Der Hund ist braun.

die Kuh

Die Kuh ist braun.

Rosa

der Kuchen

Der Kuchen ist rosa.

der Hut

Der Hut ist rosa.

Weiß

die Milch

Die Milch ist weiß.

der Schnee

Der Schnee ist weiß.

Schwarz

die Katze

Die Katze ist **schwarz**.

der Regenschirm

Der Regenschirm ist **schwarz.**

Dictionary

German Word	How To Say It	English Word
Apfel	ap-foll	apple
Banane	ba-na-nah	banana
blau	blou	blue
Blume	bloo-mah	flower
braun	brown	brown
Buch	boo-kh	book
das	duss	the (neuter)
der	der	the (masculine)
die	dee	the (feminine)
Erdbeere	ert-bear-ah	strawberry
Fisch	fish	fish
gelb	gelp	yellow
grün	groon	green
Hund	hoont	dog
Hut	hoot	hat
ist	i-sst	is

German Word	How To Say It	English Word
Karotte	ca-rot-tah	carrot
Katze	cat-zah	cat
Kuchen	koo-khen	cake
Kuh	koo	cow
Milch	meelkh	milk
orange	o-rangah	orange
Regenschirm	reagan-sheerm	umbrella
rosa	row-sa	pink
rot	roat	red
Schnee	sh-neah	snow
schwarz	sh-wartz	black
T-shirt	t-shirt	T-shirt
Tasse	tass-ah	cup
Vogel	fo-guel	bird
weiß	wheye-ss	white

See words in the "How To Say It" columns for a rough guide to pronunciations.

Index

Notes for Parents and Teachers

In German, nouns always begin with a capital letter. Nouns are also either masculine, feminine, or neuter. The word for "the" changes accordingly—so either der (masculine), die (feminine), or das (neuter).